T0195063

LOST
Moments

HANNAH ALTAIR

WESTBOW
PRESS®
A DIVISION OF THOMAS NELSON
& ZONDERVAN

WestBow Press books may be ordered through booksellers or by contacting:

WestBow Press
A Division of Thomas Nelson & Zondervan
1663 Liberty Drive
Bloomington, IN 47403
www.westbowpress.com
844-714-3454

Scripture taken from the King James Version of the Bible.

ISBN: 978-1-6642-1643-3 (sc)
ISBN: 978-1-6642-1644-0 (hc)
ISBN: 978-1-6642-1742-3 (e)

Library of Congress Control Number: 2020925404

Print information available on the last page.

WestBow Press rev. date: 02/01/2021

I dedicated this book to my mother for being the light of my life and a spiritual guide. I am grateful to you for raising me well and teaching me to love, trust, and depend on God. I see you every day since you left me in 2018, and I will see you at the end of this life. I love and miss you terribly.

Mommy
1918–2018

When I was a child, I spake as a child, I understood as a child, I thought as a child: but when I became a man, I put away childish things. (1 Corinthians 13:11)

can hear her voice saying, "You were trained since you were a child to do this job. Come on, baby. Carry me. Come on, help to take me. They are not able to help you. They are not strong enough."

Snow was melting on my hair and eyelids that morning as I stood firm in the driveway. Now the snow had turned to icy water under my feet. Was the heat from my body melting the snow, or was it the warm day of that midmorning? Memories gushed through like an open floodgate, and I staggered to keep myself from falling over from the rushing flow of the water. I hadn't anyone to hold on to something or take cover; I was alone in this. Why were they not taking over this position I was facing? They were much older than me, and they had always overseen decisions when it came to her. They had left me behind because I was the youngest one.

Automatically, I had no say where they were concerned. They were the rulers of the family.

Was I in a rage? Yes! Why now did they choose to let me take the lead with this task? I wanted to shout out, Remember, I am the baby—I don't have any say in this family! The words were not coming; only strength showed up as I closed my eyes, reopened them, and looked to the heavens for guidance.

y oldest sister was on the snowy ground, where she found comfort. I assisted her to her feet and into the arms of her brother. He pushed her in the house with his mop that was transformed into a Swiss Guard sword. She was the second child and the first daughter, and they shared everything. She was the selected ruler over us. So where was this great ruler, the mother of us, now? She crumbled to the ground. Screams, sounds of horses galloping in the house, and heads peeking from all sides of the windowpane trying to find their own space to call their own and capture the end of what was a power struggle. Not even she was there for me. My soul was relieved, and I was at peace with her leaving. I had no tears, only peace, knowing she was out of there and within the arms of the one who loved her more. No more control of whom she could see, or whom she could call, or who could call her, or whom she could visit.

How could I miss her now when I had missed her for four years?

I was in full armor. I had taken the lead down the driveway and through the open, white iron gate that I had opened on many happy occasions when I came to visit and park my SUV for safety overnight. God, how time went by so quickly. So many changes. I tried capturing a glimpse or two of a great time here, but all I could think about was the last four years of agony.

My niece was at the other end as we rolled her body through the gate and into the undertakers' van. I felt numb and was not thinking about what I was doing. I knew only that I was doing it. If I calculated correctly, I should not have been here at this time. My train would have left the station around nine thirty today, and I would have been here around two thirty to three o'clock. But I had to get out the night before because of the nor'easter, and they canceled all flights, trains, and busses. That was the reason I was standing here, closing this van with my mother's body in it. I was still listening to hear the screams coming from within myself or stamping and crushing the heads of the undertaker crew who came to take her away from me. But all I said was, "Thank you, God. Help me, God!" I looked in my scriptural archive for the words of comfort. I knew the rest of her children didn't have any comfort for me.

I told the lady from the funeral home that my mother was a proud lady and she should take the utmost respect with her body. She promised that she would be the only one to attend to her. We closed the door to the van, and I touched it and said, "Okay, Mommy, don't worry. They will take you safely." The van pulled away down the street, and I watched it disappear.

A part of me was gone. I didn't feel my feet under me, but I walked back to the driveway with my niece. I did not feel my legs, but I knew they were beneath me and were in motion. Silence took me over, and I knew that was God. If I had opened my mouth, it would have been a scene, and Mommy would have disapproved.

Was I going through this? I was sure I was going to wake up and cry a little because it was a dream of Mommy's death, her children acting foolishly and screaming at the window, and the funeral parlor van taking her away. But as I made every step up the stairs, reality kicked in. I heard my heart beating very fast, but I couldn't feel anything. I was in a rage with most of her children, and I kept thinking that Mommy would not like any problems, given that her beautiful body was still warm. We needed to come together like when we were children, put our grownup selfishness aside, hold each other, and cry until the next day. But that was not the case.

My older sister, my brother, and I left the house on a good note. We said we would be back later that evening to finalize what they had arranged a few days ago for the funeral. I sat in the backseat of my brother's car with my head facing the window for the eight miles to his home. We drove for miles in silence in our thoughts. I felt the light snow melting on my numb, hot face. The sun was playing peekaboo as it began to make its way out of the snowy clouds. I saw the streets where we drove on so many occasions— what a thing for us to face. I am not sure how my brother was able to drive, but he didn't get into an accident on the way to his home where Mommy had lived for many years.

Mommy was gone. How were we going to handle this loss? When Daddy passed, it was tough. It was our first death, and that was thirty-one years ago. But we had Mommy to cling to for comfort in our pain and grief. Now I was standing all alone with no one to comfort me. I was a grown orphan. We still think of Daddy, and whenever we talked or met, we would tell jokes about the things he did and said. But this was Mommy; she should be here forever. I had never lost a mother before, and I didn't know how to handle it.

What was I supposed to do? All I knew was I didn't want to go through this. This was not something I wanted. Could you give me something else? I'd accept a loss of a job, a relationship, but not my mother. I closed my eyes and shook my head, and the tears disappeared. If I cried, that meant she died and it was real. If I didn't cry, then she was not gone. Isn't it amazing how your emotions can confuse and restrain you when you are in a crisis?

y thoughts kept reflecting on my childhood, when she and I took long walks to visit her elderly friends from her church. We talked and laughed all the way. She was hilarious and had a great sense of humor. Then I went to my adulthood and my wedding, and how she and I designed my dress and chose the materials for our friend to make. We chatted, laughed, and sang while we baked ten pounds of wedding cake. I wanted those days to return. I wanted a magic wand or a clock to turn back time. Could I ask God to turn back the sundial like he did for Hezekiah and take me back to those days?

I was not able to see my mother in the years that she needed my warm hugs, and for me to caress her cheeks, hold her hands, and watch westerns and old movies. My blood was hot, and my breath released hot vapors; I couldn't hear my heartbeat. Was I dying? I tried to speak to my sister and brother from the backseat, but the words did not come out. And if they did, they would not have been audible or made any sense. I wanted to cry, scream, anything—yet nothing happened. In every old lady I saw on the road, I saw Mommy, especially those with beautiful winter hats. She was a stylish lady. I looked up into the heavens and squeezed my eyes tightly.

I didn't hear them in the front seat asking me if I was all right until the third time asked. I softly said, "Yes, I am," with no emotions. I asked them if they were okay. They both replied yes. They spoke about funeral arrangements they had been discussing for the last week, contacting the minister, setting the date, and developing the program.

All through the ride, until we got to my brother's home, I never spoke. All I could think about was that Mommy was taken away to the funeral home, and I wished I could have been there to see them take care of her. People say if you want to see people for who they are, have a funeral or a wedding. Well, I knew about weddings, and now I knew about funerals, and that was a big bang. I sat by the living room window listening to my sister talking to other siblings and looking over her notes she had made previously with the other family members. My brother poured us glasses of wine. The sun was shining bright, and the sky was blue. It turned into a beautiful, sunny day. Blessed, are you, God.

They were both very busy with the phone calls coming in and making calls to friends, updating them of Mommy's passing. It turned my stomach just thinking of the word *passing*. I thought about friends we knew who had died and wondered whether their children felt the same way. Somehow, I was enlisted into the drafting of the obituary and other arrangements.

My sister remembered that Mommy did not like cut flowers; she said that she was going to make a wreath using her favorite colors, and I was happy to hear that someone remembered.

That was very important to her; she said that she preferred to see them grow in the garden and not be cut. Most of her life, I never sent her flowers but would send books, shoes, hats, chocolate, and nuts. As she aged, it became difficult to read small prints, and I wanted to send her e-books, but no one would have been able to help her. Therefore, I sent large font crossword books.

We were so busy with calling contacts, writing, and editing the obituary with pen and paper that we forgot to eat, and it was now dark and time for me to check into the hotel. I realized that I had not slept since the day before and needed to rest before I fainted. I told my sister that she could stay with me at the hotel because I had two beds, and she agreed. My brother had his wife to keep his company and console him.

Before going directly to my hotel, we went to the home Mommy lived in to be with the other siblings and discuss the service and the after-burial reception. I was still silent on the way back. I thought that Mommy had left us just hours ago, and I wondered how I would feel walking back into the house. By this time, my sister had lost her voice due to crying, and I still didn't know how my brother was able to drive. I prayed for travelling mercies going and coming.

We rang the bell, and a small child came and opened the door. As we entered, we said, "Good night." A return mumble of "Good night" came from the one who sat in Mommy's chair at the window. I guess she was the one on lookout to see when we were in sight and sound the alarm.

The home was dark, with dim light coming from the living room, and we heard voices. No one came to greet us at the door, and I was very cautious because I knew deep in my spirit that something was amiss. It didn't feel right! I felt like I was watching a movie something scary was about to happen, and we were clueless to what was going on. I was very disappointed because it was time for us to unite and cuddle each other in our grief. Maybe sing a few hymns and ask God for his strength to bring us through this horrible situation. Instead, we stood at the door, lost and confused. But while we were gone for those few hours, all plans had changed. Even though it was a difficult time for us, we needed to discuss the next steps.

The look on my oldest sister's face led me to believe that she hadn't a clue what was about to go down. Calmly she said, "We said that we were coming back this evening to discuss the arrangements." The one sitting in the chair at the window turned her head and continued to look out.

The other from the living room bolted into the kitchen where we were still standing. She came like a tiger, ready to devour her prey. She said, "We will not have it on the weekend. That is our Sabbath. It is going to be on Friday."

Our older sister almost collapsed with this

new development. She asked, "When did this change? It was already discussed and agreed that it would be on the weekend. People have to work, and others have to travel from abroad and other parts of the country."

I could not believe what I was hearing, but I was still silent and looking around with a feeling of uneasiness because today was the first time I had heard of this. Everything had turned upside down.

Quickly I turned to the door and said, "Good night." My sister and brother said good night and followed me. That was darkness, and it was not of God. I prayed for covering and protection as I walked down the driveway and into the car, and I never looked back.

Back in the car, we did not speak until we got to the hotel, which was ten minutes away. It was time to order my favorite meal from the chef at the hotel restaurant. But before I did, I checked in and gave them a piece of my mind regarding them messing up my reservations.

They gave me a discount and three of my favorite hot chocolate cookies as a pacifier, which I ended up sharing with my siblings. How could I not share when they kept looking directly at my hands? They both ordered the same meal I had, the eggplant parmesan with lots of cheese and hot peppers and a little spaghetti. The chef knew exactly how I liked it, and he never disappointed me.

After booking our prospective trip back home by Amtrak for the next day, we continued making calls. That was a task because we had to keep repeating ourselves. Hard as it was, we tried not to dwell on what had just taken place at the house. My sister was in the shower for fifteen minutes, and I know that she was crying because she came out smelling like the hotel shower gel. I almost asked if she had left any for me, but when I looked at her, her eyes were puffy and red. I pained for her. She had known Mommy when she was very young and saw her age. She did a lot with and for Mommy as she was growing, and she had a great responsibility watching out for her little sisters and brothers. We were all in pain and finding our comfort in thoughts, prayers, or whatever helped us. When she opened her mouth to say it was my turn, her voice was hoarse. I thanked God we were there for each other, and we both needed a good night's rest. I was tired from the long journey the day before and the episode at the house. I am not sure when I dropped off to sleep, but I knew I rested.

The next morning after breakfast, we checked out, shared a cab, and got on Amtrak fifteen minutes apart, so she and I left Chicago around the same time and headed for our home to make arrangements to return for the burial.

walked into my home, dropped my carry-on to the floor, took off my shoes, and took a shower. I was not myself. I found myself walking around my home in the middle of the day wearing my nightgown. I must have walked into every room and was not sure why. I was trying to make sense out of all that was going on and what went wrong. I thought about this accreditation and what I needed to do to get ready, checking work e-mail and returning calls. The kettle was whistling, and I let it go for about three minutes. I wanted it to drown the thoughts I was having about that house Mommy lived with and the people's behavior. I was working on getting that vision out of my mind.

Given their behavior, I knew trouble was ahead. The sign on the road read, "Slippery when wet, and watch for falling rocks." I was still waiting on my tears to flow, but so far only a light flow trickled from my left eye. I sat for a while looking out to the ocean of snow and ice, trying to gather my thoughts. In the background, I could hear the old tunes and hymns playing. I must have drunk the whole pot of bush tea my friend had brought from Africa when she came to visit. I made another pot, and while I sat looking out, I felt her presence. I didn't have the gift to see, but I knew she was right there with me.

I began to speak to Mommy about the way I felt and how much I missed her. I complained to her about her children. I didn't sob, but this time tears flowed down my cheeks. I choked up with grief, and sorrow took hold of me. As I looked up and prayed out to God, I asked him to carry me through this storm I was in, and I crawled into his bosom and went to sleep.

When I woke, I was in my bed and under the sheet, not sure when I made it to bed. Last I remembered, I was sitting at the window.

They had booked a DJ for the reception, and I was asked to make a list of Mommy's favorite songs. Finally they included me, but that was a tough assignment. I didn't want to think about our songs at this time. They were sentimental. Her other children were always in charge of music selections for events. Why not now?

To tell you the truth, I was not functioning too well, and I had to now focus on my business when I should be grieving. I opened the door of my office to find piles of papers and binders on the desk and floor. I thought that a whirlwind had to have caused this. This was not my office. The plants were neglected, and they seemed to be yellow due to lack of water. I dropped my purse on the chair, took the containers, and watered the dying plants. Once they were fed and satisfied, I made a cup of coffee and began to work. I never stopped working on updating policies and procedures and reading instructions from the accrediting company. It took all of my thoughts and strength, and my grieving was put on the back burner.

While I worked twenty-four seven in my office, I was helping to write the program for the church service and was still making a list of her songs. Only God kept me on my feet and gave me a sound mind because by now, I should have lost it. I was still functioning and keeping up with my task. Some days I did not want to get out of bed. I wanted to be left alone. But every time I told myself that I was going to take time for myself and cry, something came up that needed my time. The last thing I heard was that the burial would be on Friday, the twenty-third.

With my flight booked, I sent the list of songs, the draft service program, and the list of Mommy's hymns with their input. Finally my tasks were accomplished. Then the drama escalated, and I kept far away from it, focused on my work, and prayed that Mommy would be laid to rest soon with her husband, Then I would come back and continue with my life.

I had a difficult time packing. The funeral was in two days, and I was trying to hold it together. I had to stand firm and trust that

God would bring me through. The luggage was packed and in the corner of the guest room, and the last thing I packed was the dress for the service. Somehow, I kept taking things out of my luggage and putting them back; this happened a few times. I began to sob for the very first time, and I said, "Mommy, I can't do this. I don't want to do this. I tried to prepare myself all my life for this day, and now it is here, and I can't deal with it."

All of a sudden, I heard her voice said, "I remember you." I burst into tears and could not stop. Then I thought of the words she said. They were also the title of one of our favorite songs that we enjoyed singing, and we would hit the high notes like the singer.

After pulling myself together and drying my long-awaited tears, I opened my computer and began to look for the song and the artist, and I found him: Slim Whitman. Don't ask me how I did it, but I played it, and as it played, I heard her singing. Oh, how I loved to listen to her sing. The lyrics of the song were perfect for my time of need. God always finds a way to reach us when we are in need. He shows us over and over again how much He loves us. He thinks about us, and he hears our cries and or thoughts. Dear heavenly Father, I cannot do this without your strength. Please guide me through this horrible and heart-wrenching time of my life. I am alone now. Take me safely to lay my dear mother to rest, and bring me back safely. Hold her in your bosom and let her know how much I love her. Tell her I miss her dearly. Lord, keep me resilient for Mommy. Help me remain silent through the funeral, and protect me from evil seen and unseen. Help me to forgive them for the unnecessary things that they have chosen to do at this time.

As expected, my siblings were on their best behavior, and Mommy's little angels for the duration of the service. She had a fair number of friends who attended, but not as many as if it were on the prior date, to allow people to travel. The phones were blowing up with calls and missed calls from friends saying how sorry they were that they were not able to attend. They wanted us to know that Mommy and Daddy made a difference in their lives and had been there when they were in need.

A few of us waited at the door of the church in anticipation. The dreaded moment came when the hearse would pull up to the curbside carrying our precious mother.

Mommy attended a small, beautiful old church that did not have an elevator, and when she was not able to walk up the stairs, they installed a chairlift. People were greeting us, crying and giving their sympathy. That did not help me, and I bit my lips. I anxiously awaited Mommy's arrival. It was a cold day, and the street was busy with shoppers, buses, and cars. Even though the sun was shining bright, I wore a full-length coat, boots, and scarf, and I was still cold. I walked back and forth to the door to keep warm. I kissed and hugged so many people and didn't know many of them, but I knew the older ones knew very well and greeted them with love. I was happy that they were able to come due to the change in date.

I ran to meet the hearse as soon as I saw it. My heart leapt within me, and I closed my eyes tightly for fear of bursting into tears, but once again I forced them away. I heard Mommy's words telling me I could do this, that I was born for this. I covered my mouth with my hand as though I was keeping a scream from escaping. She lay in a beautiful ice-blue casket, and I saw many floral wreaths from friends. All of a sudden, I thought about how Mommy felt about cut flowers, and I surprised myself with a smile. "Oh, Mommy, they brought you safely to the church," I muttered.

We had many hands, including mine, helping to take her out of the hearse. That was when I realized how heavy it was, but I was not giving up. Now it was time to take her up the stairs and into the sanctuary, and to this day I don't know how we were able to take her up and bring her back down without the casket falling over. I think that was my biggest fear on my mind for the duration of the service.

It took me a while to walk up to view her body. I was afraid and didn't know why. I kept staring at her lying there from my seat, with clasped hands under my chin and wide eyes. Her children were screaming and wailing over her, and it was harrowing to see. I blocked out and didn't want to focus. Yes, I understood that they were all grieving in their own way, as was I, but I needed to be alone.

Later, I made my way up to see her. Oh how beautiful she looked in her light blue dress and white gloves. Her hair was pure silver, and I stood there playing with her lock. I said, "You look beautiful, Mommy," and I kept looking at her. No one came to stand with me at the time, and I was glad to be there by myself. She looked great, like when I saw her last, sleeping in bed; we had both fallen asleep holding hands. I was still her baby, and I always would be! I said, "God bless your soul, Mommy. Thank you for everything."

The service was beautiful. The program information had changed, and people who were not listed in the draft were now on the program, but it was lovely and with taste. Mommy would have loved it. Her children sang and played her favorite songs and classical pieces. I don't know how they were able to do it, because I could not open my mouth to sing; this was not something I wanted to do or could have done. The minister did a fantastic job and shared many anecdotes. She spoke about visiting Mommy once a month for communion, and how she would always have two envelopes, one with tithes and another offering for the women's program— not to mention lunch, and a takeaway bag of pastries. Mommy made sure if she could not get to the house of the Lord to give her tithes, and she always kept in an envelope until a later date.

Reflections opened to friends and family, and I walked up to the altar and took out a letter from my purse that my parents' third child had written for her mother. She could not attend the service due to family dynamics, and she asked me to read it. I greeted the guests and said good morning to Mommy. I read the note and then walked back to my seat with no facial expression. I still had no feelings, just grief.

I was delighted to greet many family members whom I hadn't seen in a while, and it was good to see the new members. The church was cold, and as soon as I got back to my seat, I put on my coat and fastened the buttons. Within a few minutes the chill was gone, and I was able to feel my fingers. My daughter and I held hands while family and friends made their way slowly to the altar to say their goodbyes to

Mommy, and they made incredible speeches, giving their anecdotes.

We got her back in the hearse safely, thank God. I couldn't wait to get into the warm limo and drink a bit of water. My lips were parched, and I couldn't drink too much to keep running to the ladies' room, which felt like a mile away from the sanctuary. While we were talking about the excellent service and congratulating them for a job well done, we also spoke about Mommy's one-hundred-year-old friend and how great she looked. We enjoyed seeing her and her being there for us at this time. While sipping on the water, I asked how long it would take to come back to the reception because those who were not able to go to the cemetery would need to eat soon. That was when someone said, "Oh, the others will not be joining us at the reception. They are returning to their homes after the cemetery."

I said, "But I thought that was the reason

we had to change the date to accommodate the Sabbath."

Then someone stated that they had to prepare for their Sabbath. I shook my head in disbelief.

ymns rang out under the brilliant sun as we stood by the freshly dug grave to lay my mother's body to rest. Daddy's tombstone was there, and I felt my gut roll. I kept looking up like I was about to expect heaven to open up and everything to be different. All I kept thinking was how blue and clear the sky was, just like the day they took her body to the funeral home. The sun came out brilliantly and warmed up the day so I didn't need to wear my coat. They must have sung a fourth hymn that I did not know.

As I stood at the side of the casket, my mouth opened up, and out came words that made sense, and I recognized that it was my voice. I said, "You do not know this, but Mommy and I danced from the time I was five years old, and she taught me all her songs. Yesterday, when I was packing and repacking my suitcase, I was having a difficult time. Then I heard her voice. She said, 'I remember you.' It was one of the songs that she and I sang, so I am going to play it and dance for Mommy."

I didn't look at anyone. "This song is for my Mommy and me." With cell phone in hand lifted high above my head and pointing to the heavens, I played our song while I danced the way we always did. My heart was bursting, but I was dancing and singing for my mommy.

The pain of losing someone you truly loved is unbearable. At that moment, I wished I didn't have any feelings. You cannot take a pill or have surgery to remove feelings. It gets better with time. Time is the master for healing any pain. All I knew was it was going to be a journey ahead of me, and I began thanking God and praying for it to get better with time.

When I walked into my home after the longest train ride, I stood inside the door, and my spirit stirred up. That small voice said, "Guard your heart. You have to get back to work."

It was almost two years since she passed,

and I was still struggling with my loss. I couldn't speak with any of my siblings about this because I would hear, "Mommy is in a better place and enjoying heaven." Whenever I said something that I did with Mommy, before I finished my sentence, I was interrupted with, "If I tell you the things that Mommy and I did, you weren't born yet!" I was told that they knew everything about Mommy.

Why were they still competing even after she was gone? It was bad enough when she was alive, and I thought now she was gone, it would get better, but it did not. The tug-of-war for Mommy's love was still alive and kicking even though they were not children any longer but were grandparents themselves. I decided not to tell them how I felt, and I kept everything inside of me and worked twenty-four seven. Other than talking to God and Mommy, there were times when I needed to speak to a human being, so I would call my prayer partner. We would praise the Lord, we would laugh, and I would tell her things about Mommy. She would say, "Your mommy was a Proverbs 31 woman, and she was very wise."

Indeed, Mommy was. She was the best.

Work was not easy. Dealing with insurance companies, clients, and working on accreditation for my business was a struggle, but God was able. I prayed, fasted, cried over the work, and cried for the loss of Mommy all at the same time. Yet I did not give myself time to grieve. I kept telling myself, "No time to grieve now. I will grieve later. I am going to take a trip and sit on a beach and cry, eat, and sleep." I wanted to be far away in a place where I didn't have to think, answer questions, or see anyone. But I had to prepare for the surveyor and get full accreditation. The state wanted my business to be accredited within the year; if not, they would cancel my contract. That did not sit well with me. It was so much work to complete, and the red tape was a mile away, but what could one expect from the government? The clients depended on this program, and I knew I had to keep it going. The need was great, and they needed a voice and someone to fight for them. Even though I didn't feel like a fighter, this was something I needed to do for me. I worked too hard, and through my tears, I kept seeing the light at the other side of the mountain.

The Lord is my light and my salvation; whom shall I fear? The Lord is the strength of my life; of whom shall I be afraid. (Psalm 27:1)

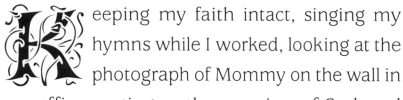eeping my faith intact, singing my hymns while I worked, looking at the photograph of Mommy on the wall in my office, resting on the promises of God, and persevering was my ticket to my future. Nothing came easily. If it did, then one would not enjoy it when it happened. The test was wrapped up in the promise. Through my life, I could look back and see that the disappointments, setbacks, stalling, and uncertainties were for a reason. I was in training camp, learning everything that I would need for where I was today and where God was taking me. My mother was cheering me on, and I kept seeing her smile.

We feel pain, cry, and ask God what is going on in our lives. Why are we going through what we are going through? Sometimes he tells us, and other times he is silent.

When I was much younger, I was not too fond of silence. Now that I am older, I understand the silence and I rejoice in it; this is the time to search within, pray, and wait.

We always want fast answers and quick turnarounds, but we need to stand still and enjoy the process, like making a cake. As soon as you finish mixing the batter, you wish for a slice. Forget the baking and cooling time—just cut the cake. Use that opportunity to look around your surroundings. Whom do you have walking with you, whom do you need to leave behind, and are you ready for the next level? If you are prepared, then ask God if he is ready to move you to the next level.

I find when I am on this threshold, it is something that I must do before God moves me to the next level. It's almost like a chess game. Sometimes I see my life was on this board, and I have no clue how to play chess, so I know God is winning. Whether it is comfortable or uncomfortable, I know it is for his glory.

Time is the master. The surveyor came the day of my birthday, one month before Mommy's first anniversary. I thought this must be my birthday gift in disguise. I prayed and thanked

God in advance for my three full years of accreditation. My office was intact, and desks, binders, and files were ready to be scrutinized by the surveyor. She was a well-dressed, round-faced, middle-aged lady with a beautiful smile that warmed my heart. It was a cold day with temperatures in the single digits. The office was comfortable and smelled of vanilla and honeysuckle. We introduced ourselves, made coffee, chitchatted, and then we got down to business. She began asking for items, and I pulled them out for her review. I had everything she needed. Some of the information I had needed to be edited or omitted, and other aspects had to be updated. My clients and staff were interviewed at length on the services they received from my business and work ethics. For three full days, I shared my office and was under scrutiny, but I was not worried. I knew that I was at least 90 percent on target with the policies and procedures, but I still felt pressured. Creating and developing a business alone is not easy, and it comes with sleepless nights and some fear. For those three days, it was hard not to think of Mommy, but I had to be tough and smile even though I wanted to scream, "Why do you have to be here in my office right now? Do you know that I haven't grieved yet, and I need to be alone?"

Tea and coffee kept my eyes open for the long days I worked with the surveyor, and I prayed for the last day to end. Each night I slept well and gained my strength for the next day of questioning, poking through policy and procedural binders, and making notes on her laptop while I glance up from my computer to look at her facial expression. I tried reading her face, but she had a poker face.

I wasn't sure what to think of her typing on the computer, pulling papers out of her briefcase, reading, and putting them back into her case.

She was excellent, a wonderful teacher, and she taught me a lot for the three days she spent with me. She said that she was very impressed with my ability to singlehandedly develop and run a business with everything in place. I was genuinely grateful to hear those words. I know that God was with me. He taught me all that I knew, and when I didn't know how to do certain things, I cried out and said, "God, I don't have anyone to help me. What am I going to do?" He showed me what I needed to know, and He said, "My grace is sufficient." I had made numerous calls asking for help, but everyone wanted me to pay them thousands of dollars for what God himself taught me. Hallelujah! Thank you, God, for your favor.

When she packed up her laptop on her last day, I looked up with relief and said quietly, "Thank you, God, for my accreditation."

My surveyor put on her coat, picked up her briefcase and laptop, and walked to the door. She stopped and said, "Thank you for having me and being a wonderful hostess for three days. Continue doing a great job, and I wish you success and a great future." She gave me a bright smile and walked out.

I closed the door and looked at Mommy's picture on the wall. I smiled and said, "Thank you, Mommy, for cheering me on and keeping my company all through this preparation." I sat in my chair and cried softly, and I felt the hot tears rolling down my cheeks. "Blessed are you, O God. No one knows how far I have come and how I got here. It is easy for folks to be jealous, hateful, and envy, but if they only knew." Grace brought me through. If it were not for the goodness and love of God, I would not have made it.

t was now one year since the surveyor had come to my office. This year it was different. I was going to Africa to spend time with my new family friends. I needed this more than anything. You see, last year it was a testimony, but I made it through. God showed me people who were hiding behind a veil for years, but God said it was time to expose them, and he did. It is not an easy thing to be there for people and then find out that they never cared for you. They were only walking with you because they needed you to help them out. You are always there to help even when you are busy with your own personal and professional life. You keep giving and giving, and they keep taking, using, and taking you for granted. And somehow, they think that you should do these things. There comes a time when God says, "Enough is enough." He begins to tear down the drapes, pull off the covers, and show us the real person beneath. They are wolves in sheep's clothing, smiling and laughing with you and hateful in their hearts. It was time to see them in full color, and even though I was not expecting it, God prepared me and gave me the strength to face the betrayal.

Whenever God is getting ready to take us to the next level, the enemy shows up to break our spirits and seeks for us to give up. The enemy uses family or friends to do his dirty, filthy works. We need to remember that we serve a great and awesome God who sees all things and allows things to happen in our lives to make us stronger. When these things are happening in our lives, look up, and ask God what is it that I need to learn from this.

Heart-wrenching and painful as the situation may be, our God will bring us out and give us the victory. I know that he will never leave me. Mommy always told me to trust him. Of all the things she taught me from childhood to adulthood, if I didn't remember anything else,

I remember to trust him even when it didn't make sense.

Early last year, I planned to go to Africa with few people in the spring, and I was thrilled that we were going on a well-deserved trip. I had worked hard the previous years, and it was time for me to celebrate my achievements. I was filled with joy, and I began making plans for the 2020 trip as the months progressed. God put it on my heart that I should change my spring trip and go late winter. I booked my flight, mapped out my travel plans, contacted my friends, and started packing my bags. The month before I left, I began hearing about a virus in Asia, and people had died.

I continued to pack, and I made sure that I had all my medications, hand sanitizer, masks, gloves, and scarves for travel. I needed to be away, spending time to think about my future and about Mommy. I wanted to look at my life, and to see the countries of that vast continent of Africa for the first time. I was very excited and couldn't wipe the smile off my face. It was indeed a blessing, and I was so grateful for this extraordinary season of my life.

Every other day, I contacted my friends about their weather forecast in their prospective countries, and I made adjustments in my clothing. I also had to be careful with the kilograms and pounds, because each airline had its own rules. That was tiring, frustrating, and stressful. I also planned what suitcase I would take to which country, and where I would leave the others. All of that took me a month to finalize. I also had a finicky diet, so I investigated the foods in all the countries. I was worried that if I didn't pack noodles, crackers, trail mix, fruit bars, and protein bars, I would starve in a few of the countries. All the dishes I kept seeing were starch and game. I realized that few of the countries I would stay in the least would have my kind of meals in abundance. I knew that I would consider this factor for the next trip.

Staff and client projects were all set for the month. I had excellent staff, and they worked with such diligence and were trustworthy and dependable. I had no worries about anything going wrong, and if so, I could still be reached by e-mail. Nevertheless, I was not worried. My accountant had it all under control, and the weekly payroll would be done on schedule every Monday morning before ten o'clock. I held staff meetings twice before I left to iron out anything that needed to be addressed before my departure, and I worked long hours in the office and at home. I cleaned the office desks and windows, took out rubbish, watered the plants, and filed all paperwork in their designated places. I even cleaned the refrigerator and coffee maker. I wanted to leave the office spotless for my staff so they could continue keeping the office clean with everything in place. Before I left the office, I walked through twice, made sure the windows were closed, went over to Mommy's picture on the wall, and stood there for a while, smiling. I was ready for my trip.

I had passport and boarding pass. I wore a hat, gloves, a face mask, and a scarf, and I had supply of hand sanitizer and everything I could think of to kill germs. I was ready to see Southern Africa. I stood in line and envisioned the places I would see face-to-face. Weeks before I traveled, I looked on YouTube to see the sites of places that I had on my list. I must have had a smile on my face for so long because when I got to the counter, the woman said, "You are happy." I said yes, because I was on my way to Africa. She asked where I was going and told me to have a great trip and a safe journey.

The flight was not the greatest to France; they said I had too many toiletries in my carry-on, and they should be in a Ziploc bag. When she showed me the size, I almost passed out. I said, "What? That bag?" I asked her what women she knew would carry that bag with toiletries. I didn't think even men carried a bag with shaving cream, comb, razor, makeup, and whatever they were using today. It was the favor of God that she did not take them away. She warned me that when I came through again, they would throw away the excess items. But what she didn't know was that I was taking a direct flight home. I had such a difficult time in France and with Air France that I vowed to not travel that route ever again—not forgetting the meals of cheese and bread, cheese and bread, bread and cheese, and a lot of cream sauce and milk. Hello! I was lactose intolerant.

t was late night when we landed, and from the sky it was magical. I could have flown around for another hour looking at the landscape of twinkling lights of many colors.

What a beauty. I was in southern Africa. I held my heart and closed my eyes. I was finally here in this great land of my ancestors, and there was so much joy.

The lady behind the counter asked where I was coming from and why was I there. I told her with a bright smile that I was from the United States, and I was here to spend a month and celebrate an early birthday. I also told her to make sure that the stamp was bright and bold. She laughed and stamped the red ink pad twice before stamping my passport. She said, "Welcome to South Africa. Enjoy your stay, and be safe."

I said, "I will, thank you!" I pulled my carry-on and put a large handbag over my shoulder that was filled with snacks, medication, hand sanitizer, masks, sweater, and the scarf that kept me warm on the flight. I was now sweltering, but I yearned for the heat. I left the cold, snow, heavy boots, hats, and gloves behind me, and I traded it for sundresses and sandals.

My friend Lani was waiting for me as I walked out with two large suitcases, carry-on, and handbag. She ran toward me, and we embraced for about a minute. Then we began jumping, hugging, and laughing with joy. Oh, what a moment that was. I was so happy to see her. She helped me with the luggage, and we walked to her SUV. She jokingly asked if I was in Africa for two months instead of two weeks.

I always overpacked. This time was different, and I packed wisely Instead of seven or ten pairs of shoes, I packed only five, including one pair of hiking boots that I was wearing. We were en route to my hotel, and I was tired from the fifteen hours of travel. I was wide-eyed and took in the scenery. The sky was bright blue with a few puffs of clouds, the moon was full, and the stars greeted me. What a beautiful night it was, quiet and peaceful. I almost thought I was dreaming, but it was real. Even if I painted it, it would not have been as beautiful as what I saw. I looked at Lani and said, "Am I really here?" She reached for my hand and smiled while nodding. We were both choked up with tears. It had been three years since I had seen her, and being with her again was such a delight. She was a beautiful friend, prayerful, loved the Lord, and cared for her patients. She had a heart of gold, was soft-spoken and petite, yet she could have hoisted a mountain through her faith.

The hotel staff came, stacked the luggage onto the trolley, and rolled it into the lobby. We made our way to the front desk and checked in. I asked if the restaurant was open. The man at the counter said it closed at eleven o'clock. I looked at my watch, and it was now 1:00 a.m. He went on to say that the bar was open, and they may have something I could get from the kitchen. We made our way quickly and asked a young man if they would be able to make me a dish. He asked me what I wanted to eat. I told him I didn't know and would need to look at a menu. I quickly ran through it and made a simple selection of fish and chips. He told me that the chef would make it for me, and it would be ready within fifteen minutes.

Lani and I went up to the room with the attendant and luggage. When the door opened, I almost fell over. The room was vast and beautiful. There were big windows that opened to a balcony, and the big open ocean was in view with the moon shining in my face. There was a light ocean breeze. I was beyond happy! I felt so blessed and grateful for what God had done for me. All of this was for me.

I bade Lani good night and told her to call when she got home. Then I made my way to get my late dinner and a bottle of wine. I thought it was a beautiful hotel, and it was very safe, secured, and gated—all pluses for me. The rooms were amazing, and from what I had experienced, they had great staff.

I sat on the balcony, ate my dinner, and drank my wine. It was about 2:30 a.m., and I was still up to enjoy the view. I didn't want to go to sleep. The sky was so bright that I was sure if I looked hard and long, I would have seen heaven. This had to be real; it could not have been a dream. If it had been a dream, I would have been furious. With tears in my eyes, I softly said, "Thank you, heavenly Father, for not forgetting me."

I took it in: the full moon shining brightly onto the ocean, the silence of the night, the stars twinkling. I tried to make a video, but when I viewed it, it was not the same. I think God himself was saying, "This one is on me—not for sale!" I tossed the camera to the side, closed the balcony door, and lay in my bed to fall asleep with the moon in my face. I felt as one with the night, and I didn't want to part with it.

Not in a million years had I thought I was going to be here, now, in this place. I knew that I was tired and had a long journey, but my spirit was happy, and I could not stop smiling and even laughing out and lifting my wine glass in thanksgiving. I must have giggled myself to sleep. This trip was unbelievable.

I would not be able to explain what I saw in Africa. I took many photographs, but this beauty must be for the naked eye. I climbed the sand dunes and drew a heart on the way up dune seven. Inside it I wrote, "Thanks, God." Another ten feet up, I made two hearts, one with my parents' initials and the other one with mine and a flower. It was a quiet early Sunday morning, and I sat there for a while and looked out into the distance, at the hands of God. I felt such peace and at the same time a sadness while thinking of Mommy and Daddy. I wished they had made this trip to see this beautiful land. Such beauty all around me—mountains, hills, ocean, animals, birds, people. I choked up with emotions.

I will lift up my eyes unto the hills, from whence cometh my help. My help cometh form the Lord which made heaven and earth. (Psalm 121:1)

very country I visited had its own beauty, to the point that I didn't want to return home. If I could have switched countries and my job, I would have done it in an instant. I was overwhelmed with beauty. It was an emotional roller coaster. I saw the hand of God on every hill and every mountain. Indeed, he is excellent! Every time I looked up, I thought of Psalm 121,s Mommy's favorite. I was now a different person. I was more focused on what was essential and what must be done.

Spending precious time with my friends was a blessing. Every day, early in the morning when I woke, I went to the window of my hotel, looked up, and thanked God for his goodness, favor, and blessings in my life. "You didn't forget me, Lord. Thank you so much for what you have done for me, what you are doing for me, and what you are about to do for me. I am genuinely grateful to you, Lord. I pray about this coronavirus that I hear about, and I ask you to protect us and bless someone with the knowledge to find a cure. They said that a few people died, and I am not sure what to think about it. But take charge, Lord, and protect us. Thank you. I love you, Lord. Amen."

We traveled to many bordering countries and ate exciting foods. I even tried mopane worm stew. They were edible caterpillars that fed off of the mopane tree. They were said to be high in protein. If I ever ran out of food, I knew what I was going to be eating.

Even though COVID-19 had begun to escalate on my trip, I diligently applied my hand sanitizer, wore my mask and gloves, wiped down everything in sight on and off the planes, and checked my temperature. They took my temperature at every checkpoint at the airports in Africa, and somehow I was not afraid about the virus, only cautious. I prayed all through my trip until I came back. I was surprised that when I got back to America, they did not check my temperature; they simply asked if I had a fever and if I had been in China in the last two weeks. I answered no and went my way.

I was not sure what to make of this plague, but it was severe, and it was taking many lives. I kept abreast of all news channels and followed all procedures. What was it that we needed to learn from this? I was glad that Mommy was resting in the arms of God. She would have been so distraught, crying for the world. I thought about my healing and things I wanted to tell Mommy. We always wrote letters, and when her friends wrote to her, she would call me and read their letters to me. We enjoyed letter writing.

At the end, Mommy was frail and dependent on having the family members she lived with to dial the phone numbers for her. If her phone was around her and the volume was not turned down, she would have been answering her phone and taking calls from her other children and the few friends she had left. That was not the case. Now power, control, dictatorship, and evil rained down. My mother was in her nineties. Most of her peers had already gone home to be with the Lord. The fight was gone from her, and she was preparing to meet her maker. Even though I did not get to see Mommy for four years due to family dynamics, we spoke on the phone, and every time we spoke, I had to say to her, "Why is the television so loud while you are speaking to me? I can't hear you. Can you have someone turn it down?" She would call someone and ask them to turn it down, even though I heard loud voices around her, so they should know that she was on the phone and they should keep their voices low. She kept saying to me, "I can't hear you. What did you say?" I kept shouting and hurting my vocal cords to speak over all the noise surrounding her.

The last year, her hands were feeble, and it was difficult for her to dial the numbers. So, she depended on others, but once she was on the phone, her voice was strong and engaging. Mommy's hands were now weak, and she needed assistance in dialing the phone and even walking. Her mind was sharp as a razor, and 95 percent of her memory was intact. She was still able to feed herself, but she ate slower than before. Because she could not make her phone calls, I had lost moments with Mommy. Sometimes I could not speak with her because no one picked up the phone when it rang.

I continued mailing large print books, cards, letters, and other usable gifts I knew she enjoyed. I was more excited when I received the notification that her packages had reached safely at her door, and I waited in anticipation to hear her voice laughing and telling me how she felt about her gifts. We talked about books she read, poems she remembered and still recited. What a great memory she had. It didn't matter how small and insignificant a gift was; she was delighted and showed gratitude. I prayed and asked God not to have Mommy see what was going on around her. She had been kind to all her children and loved every one of us. As with most parents, she would have her favorites. All I knew was I was her baby. She always told me that I had always been an obedient child. I left everything in God's hands because I knew what he had done for me and what he was doing for me. My God sat high and watched low, and he knew the heart of man. He knew the evil inside us humans, the pure in heart, the haters, and those who cursed inwardly but showed bright smiles outwardly. I prayed that Mommy had peace and joy in her heart and did not see the evil that surrounded her.

For what shall it profit a man, if
he shall gain the whole world, and
lose his own soul? (Mark 8:36)

ne day while shopping at the grocery store, I ran into Lizzy. She was someone I had worked with several years ago at a publishing company. Lizzy was smart and beautiful and was always well dressed. What I remembered most of all was her love for the Lord. She left everything in his hands when she couldn't make sense of her life. Many times we shared our spiritual beliefs and journeys. As I approached her, I called her name. "Lizzy?"

She turned around, but it was not the face I remembered. That smile was not there. The invitation to communicate and laugh was not there. Instead, I found eyes that were deep and dark with circles that makeup could not hide. Her red hair was now pulled back in a ponytail, though of course she still had the red lipstick;

no matter what time of day it was, she had to have her lipstick.

She dropped her basket when she saw me, ran to me, and held my hands. I asked how she was, and she kept shaking her head. She said, "Not good" while tears poured down her cheeks. I asked if she had time to talk, and she said yes. We returned the items in our baskets to their prospective places. We walked to the cafe at the corner from the grocery store and talked over a cup of coffee.

Lizzy tried holding back tears while she shared her sad story of losing her mother. Lizzy's mother was put into a nursing home by her older brother even though their father told them if he passed away before her, they were to take care of their mother in her house or at the home of one of their three children. Lizzy was the youngest, so her two older brothers were in charge of healthcare and finances, and they kept her out of any decisions they made regarding her mother. The two brothers sold their parents' home and put their mother in a nursing home unbeknownst to Lizzy. When she told them that she should have been a part in the decision, they told her that they had legal rights to do what they wanted to do, and it had nothing to do with her. What the brothers did not sell, they divided among themselves and their families.

One day the second born called and told Lizzy that he was coming to her office to take her out for lunch. Lizzy said that they laughed and talked, and she enjoyed the time she spent with him. She said this was the brother whom she was always bailing out of financial crisis when he moved from one state to the next. He had drained her for years, but she didn't mind. She loved her brother and was always there for him, but during those years, he took her for granted and abused her kindheartedness.

She straightened up, and took a few sips of her coffee, and looked around. Through a strained smile, she said, "While we were at lunch that very day, laughing and talking, my mother had been admitted to the hospital the day before. He knew and never said a word to me."

"What"?

"Yes. My brother looked me straight in the face and never said a word. That is the epitome of evil."

"I am so sorry, Lizzy."

She blinked away the tears and continued. "When it was my mother's eighty-eighth birthday, they did not tell me that they had planned a party the day before her birthday at the nursing home. When I showed up the morning of her birthday with a small cake from her favorite bakery, gifts, and a balloon, the staff asked where I had been the day before. I asked them, 'What happened yesterday?' They told me that my brothers and their families were there to celebrate her birthday, and they had brought a cake for staff and residence.

"When she died, my brothers took charge

of the funeral arrangements, and they asked if I wanted to be on the program. I declined. I asked them about the reception after the service. My brothers told me that they were not going to have one because they didn't want to feed anyone—they needed the money, and it was a waste of time."

"What?" I could not believe what I was hearing.

"Yes, that was their response, even though they had taken so much already—the sale of the house, her jewels, and anything they could have put their hands on. Yet couldn't honor her with an after-service reception." Lizzy was pouring out her soul, and all I could do was listen.

Before Lizzy left, she turned and said, "We are a small family. I don't have other relatives, and I have been suffering in isolation for a long time. If I don't understand anything else in the scriptures, I know that I serve a just God! Before you take time to do evil, do good."

I didn't tell Lizzy about my experience with my mother's birthday. A few years ago, I traveled the month of her birthday and could not speak with her to wish her a happy birthday. While I was away, I found out that they had a party and invited many people, including people from out of state, but no one shared that information with me. For the four years I did not see her, I was closer to her than ever. I am not sure how to explain it, but it was the way I felt right now. It was amazing. This experience was unbelievable. I wanted to listen to Lizzy because she needed to talk and had no one; my story could wait for another time. Many families faced division, and my family wasn't excluded from this verse in the Bible: "For from henceforth there shall be five in one house divided, three against two and two against three" (Luke 12:52).

The Lord watch between me and thee, when we are absent one from another. (Genesis 31:49)

ur heartstrings got tighter and tighter, and it would always be that way. I truly adored Mommy from the day I met her; she was my queen, and in many ways she was the best thing that happened to me. I prayed, "Thank you, God, for choosing me as her youngest child. I am truly blessed to have been raised by her. What a gift!"

When I last saw Mommy, I kneeled by her bedside and told her not to worry about my daughter and me. I told her to remember that God always took care of us, and he would continue. She could not speak but mumbled and nodded. I keep rubbing her hands gently and telling her that we would be fine. Others may have gone through what I had gone through, but this was one of the hardest things for me, knowing that my mother was leaving me behind. I wanted to scream, "Don't you leave me!"

This was the road that we all will take, but she would always tell me to trust him. I threw myself in his arms and held on for dear life. I never wanted to go through the loss of losing my mother. God blessed Mommy with long, strong, healthy years. And no matter how long He prepared me, it still was not easy laying her to rest. My hope is that in the end, I will embrace my Mommy and Daddy.

I decided to write Mommy one last letter because I was not able to do so in the previous year of her life, telling her of the plight we were facing today. I wanted to thank her again for all she had done for me. Even though she was gone, I would not use the pet name that I called her. I would say "Mommy."

Let your light so shine before men, that they may see your good works, and glorify your Father which is in heaven. (Matthew 5:16)

My dearest Mommy,

I pray that this letter finds you in good health, strength, love, and joy, and in sound mind. God has truly blessed you with a ripe old age, and I know that you are even amazed to see that you have lived so long on this earth.

I know that the world has changed since you graced this earth with your presence in 1918, and God keeps you in every way of your life. You shared with me so often that you never thought you would have lived so long to see eighty years, and now it's ninety-nine years. How many of us will be able to see those years and still have a sound mind and no disease? Not everything was the way you wanted it to be; you had many dreams that did not manifest in your life. But you were still so thankful for God's goodness, and you proved that your whole life. It is suitable for children to see parents such as you; it gives us hope in the Lord and to know that we do not receive everything we want.

God knows what to give every one of us, and we have to seek understanding, though hard it may be at times; we are human, and we have desires. Nevertheless, you were thankful. Besides you, if I had to choose any woman in the world to be my mother, I would not accept any. You were indeed the best. You imparted such wisdom and knowledge, and I soaked it all in and on every level of my life where I apply them.

I would have given you the world if I could, and I know that you know that. You have been a true inspiration in my life and guided me in what is right and wrong. I am seeing it differently today in our nation: that what is wrong is right, and what is right is wrong. You also told me that I had worked very hard, and I will get my harvest from the Lord. I want you to know that things are going very well, and it is all about that trust you told me of so long ago.

Since you left, the world has drastically changed so that I don't recognize it. The scriptures are speaking. Those with eyes will surely see; if not, they are going to be in for a long, bumpy horseback ride without a saddle. Sad, but it is so true. We now have to deal with the COVID-19 pandemic that they said came out of China and now plagues the entire world; it causes some states to be on lockdown and orders to stay at home. Schools are closed, and nonessential people are told to work from home. Churches are closed, and we are not to have large gatherings. Restaurants and even some parks are closed to those who are not adhering to the voice of common sense.

We were told to practice social distancing as a safety precaution, and if we have to go out, we should stay six feet away from others—no handshaking nor hugging. We should wash hands with soap for twenty seconds. Well, I had to laugh because from the time we were young, we were continually washing our hands and cleaning with disinfectant, and covering our mouths with kerchief or tissue when we coughed or sneezed. People now know that doing simple childhood hygiene is essential; these were things that we were taught at an early age. Where did the training go?

As children, we couldn't come into the home with shoes; they had to be taken off at the door. That has not changed. When your older children were wearing bellbottoms in the seventies, you and Daddy told them that they could not sweep the streets and come into the home. They had to take them off at the door. You and Daddy were very strict. You had your rules, and we had to follow them. This is what people should have been doing all of their lives. How many times while shopping have we seen people use the bathroom and walk right out without washing their hands? We would always say, "Thank God we do not eat from people." Could you imagine us not holding hands and hugging? We are making face masks for ourselves if we do not have a nonsurgical cover. The younger generation, the wise and untouchable ones, are still meeting in large gatherings, getting the virus, and passing it on to others. Not only that, but they are dying. Rules are not made for them.

Only medical personnel and frontline staff, people at the grocery stores, and pharmacy personnel should be going to work, or if you have a good reason for being on the street, such as going to pick up medications or essentials. People are dropping like flies, scared stiff and depressed. The medical officials and some state governors (like New York) have been giving daily news briefs. We haven't many ventilators for patients, or gloves and masks to protect the medical staff and first responders. I have to tell you that I have not heard the names Jesus or God used so many times in the media. People are asking pastors to pray on the television. Now they remember to use the name of the Most High God. Is it only when we are in a crisis that we remember God?

Solitude is not hard for me. Others have difficult times practicing this new normal because they are so accustomed to large gatherings, meetings, and having company over. I genuinely think this is a time for people to get to know themselves and face what they see in the mirror. I believe this is the time to get to know God intimately. Social interaction is vital to humans, and I pray for the elderly who live alone, but I do believe that the more we follow the guidelines, the faster this virus will leave us. As of today, the unemployment rate is 6.6 million and rising, the global infection rate is now 1,033,478 with 54,269 deaths, and for us here in the United States, the cases are 245,601 and 6,058 deaths and counting. The senseless killings of Black men and women by police officers escalated, and we are seeing more hate and bigotry than ever before. I am crying for the world, and sometimes I get scared and wonder what will become of our world. Then I remember how great God is. In Genesis 1:26 (KJV), it is written, "And God said, let us make man in our own image, after our likeness: and let them have dominion over the fish of the sea, and over the fowl of the air, and over the cattle, and over all the earth, and over every creeping thing that creepeth upon the earth."

God have mercy on His people. As sad as it is, I thank God for taking you home when he did, because you would have been anxious for your children, grandchildren, and great-grandchildren, and in fact for the whole world. This would not have been a good thing for you to see. I try not to be afraid. I meditate on the verses of the Bible that tell me I should not fear and should stand firm and look up. I am praying daily for the world. In all things, we are to give thanks and praises to God. And at this time, I am healing more and more every day.

I saw your strength in everything you did and your perseverance through trials. I saw you sacrifice for your children. The family was everything to you. You were the glue that held us together, but some of your children invented a glue resistance, and they used it well. You were never weary of giving and helping others. You and Daddy did remarkable things for people, and you never looked back for anything.

You were always there to help a neighbor or a friend. You were the giver and the lender. Before you feed your family, if not most of the time, you will first send a meal to your neighbor, and I learned well. I am trying to carry on that torch to the end. Some days take the strength out of me, but God takes over where I am weak, and he does the rest. So often I feel your presence, and I see you smiling that beautiful smile and your large gray eyes filled with love. I can count the times when I saw you angry, and for excellent reasons. You did an awesome job raising us.

I remember the five o'clock early morning devotions, and all that you taught me, including how to pray, is needed for this day. I am working from home now, and I go out only when I have to. Sometimes I have had to make a trip to the office, which is fifteen minutes away. Thank God that I didn't have to drive a distance to be out there with this virus we cannot see. It is deadly.

If we could see it, maybe we can run from it, but this thing is in the air. We are breathing it in like mold. Only God can fight this, and I pray that He will give scientists the knowledge to find the cure; then I hope they will praise him. I am counting my blessings every day he wakes me up. I see the goodness of God. Praise his holy name.

As I am coming to grips with my loss of you, day by day as I see the death toll rises from the coronavirus, I am getting stronger and healing from my grief. I am always thinking of you but not grieving. I have already forgiven those who willfully kept you away from me for whatever reason; may God have mercy on them. I am your baby and always will be. What I remember most of all is the way you always ended your conversation with me. You would say, "Baby, I love you, I love you, I love you."

Thank you, my dear sweet mother, for your kindness in words and actions to my daughter and me, for teaching me the word of God, and for loving me unconditionally. I could not have been blessed with a better mother. I will always keep you in my heart and remember all you have taught my daughter and me.

I do feel your presence. Sometimes I wake up singing your songs after you visit me in dreams. When I listen to the oldies radio station, I try to sing our songs in entirety and not stop in the middle with crying fits. I am not fooling myself; I know it will take some time. When I hear all the songs we sang, such as "With a Song in My Heart," I hear your soprano voice. "Great Is Thy Faithfulness." "The Very Thought of You." "That Sunday, That Summer"—this one tears me apart. Or any song by Nat King Cole, and your favorite hymns. I will try to sing them.

Enjoy heaven, my dear, beautiful Mommy. Continue to cheer me on. God knows I need it, especially now. God kept me from falling, and he removed those he does not want in my life. I am so happy and grateful, I have such peace, and I am free. He told us to guard our hearts. Thanks be to God. I have to remain focused on his work and not to be sidetracked with people who do not have any good intentions for me. You are in the light I see every day, in the stars every night, and in your songs. Your spirit is always with your granddaughter and me. We will meet again, so I will say you are away for just a moment. Thank you for everything you have done for us. God bless your soul. I love you, I love you, I love you!

Your loving daughter,
The Baby

And God shall wipe away all tears from their eyes; and there shall be no more death, neither sorrow, nor crying, neither shall there be any more pain: for the former things are passed away. (Revelation 21:4)

know that you may have something to say to a loved one that you cannot see, or one you could not see and has passed away. Like my friend Lizzy, who has suffered silently in isolation. We all have our own stories to tell. We cannot measure sorrow or grief. Sometimes we can only share a few of our stories and leave the rest in the hands of God. Trust him with your pain and your sorrows. This section is for you to say how you feel about that person. It may bring you closure. Do not be afraid to write your feelings; they will help you release the pain or refresh some of your beautiful memories and moments. Give it a try. Remember that God is our healer and strength. Be blessed.

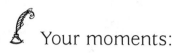 Your moments:

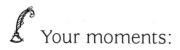 Your moments:

Printed in the United States
By Bookmasters